WHATSAID SERIF

NATHANIEL MACKEY

WHATSAID SERIF

NATHANIEL MACKEY

CITY LIGHTS BOOKS
San Francisco

Cover design by DiJit
Book design by Robert Sharrard
Typography by Harvest Graphics

Library of Congress Cataloging-in-Publication Data

Mackey, Nathaniel. 1947–
    Whatsaid Serif / by Nathaniel Mackey.
       p.   cm.
    ISBN 0-87286-341-7
    I. Title.
    PS3563.A3166W48   1998
    811'.54 — dc21
                                                              98-11042
                                                                  CIP

City Lights Books are available to bookstores through our primary
distributor: Subterranean Company, P.O. Box 160, 265 S. 5th Street,
Monroe, OR 97456. Tel.: (541)-847-5274. Toll-free orders (800)-274-7826.
Fax: (541)-847-6018. Our books are also available through library jobbers
and regional distributors. For personal orders and catalogs, please write
to City Lights Books, 261 Columbus Avenue, San Francisco, CA 94133 or
visit us on the World Wide Web at http://www.citylights.com.

CITY LIGHTS BOOKS are edited by Lawrence Ferlinghetti and Nancy J.
Peters and published at the City Lights Bookstore, 261 Columbus
Avenue, San Francisco, CA 94133.

Some of these poems first appeared in the following publications: *apex of the M, The Capilano Review, Chicago Review, Conjunctions, Ergo!, Fourteen Hills: The SFSU Review, Grand Street, Hambone, The Iowa Review, New American Writing, Phoebe, The Poetry Project Newsletter, River City, Sulfur, trembling ladders, The World.*

Song of the Andoumboulou: 18–20 was published in a limited letterpress edition by Moving Parts Press in 1994. *Strick: Song of the Andoumboulou 16–25*, a compact disc recording of the author reading section I of this book with musical accompaniment (Royal Hartigan, drums and percussion; Hafez Modirzadeh, reeds and flutes), was released by Spoken Engine Company in 1995. Both are available from Small Press Distribution, 1341 Seventh Street, Berkeley, CA 94710-1403.

*to the memory of
my brother,
Thomas Mackey
(1936–1996)*

CONTENTS

. . . in order for the story to be told at all, it must be received by a responder or "what-sayer," who is a crucial actor in the situation. The what-sayer may be someone who asked to be given the narrative or the recipient of a story that exemplifies explanatory principles needing clarification during the course of some other discussion; the person serving as what-sayer can change during the course of a telling. . .

—Ellen B. Basso, *A Musical View of the Universe*

. . . an obliquely laid arc with a straight segment on the bottom forming a hook. This is the sign of the earth in its incompleteness. . .

—Marcel Griaule and Germaine Dieterlen, *The Pale Fox*

I

STRICK

What you must search for, and find, is the black torso of the Pharaoh.

—Manuel Torre to García Lorca

SONG OF THE ANDOUMBOULOU: 16

— cante moro —

They were dredging
the sea, counting
the sand. Pounded
rocks into gravel,
paid a dollar a
day,
sang of the oldest
fish like family,
tight
flamenco strings
distraught. . .

Some
ecstatic elsewhere's
advocacy strummed,
unsung, lost inside
the oud's complaint. . .
The same cry taken
up in Cairo, Córdoba,
north
Red Sea near Nagfa,
Muharraq, necks cut
with the edge
of a
broken cup. . .
Lebrijano's
burr-throat, raspy
as night, adamant
night, long night
longer
than a lifetime of
nights. . .
Turning away what light

3

was outside, night
    without end. . .
                    Muttering,
    "Time," less than a
        sigh, resigned
    to it, would-be
                Book
of Coming Forth by Day,
                        would-be
        kef-pesh, pinkish
                        sun. . .
        Between lips, resuscitant,
                            reached
        where they were, no boat not
    one they drowned in, dredged
        it,   letterless the
    book we thumbed. . .

                        Blocked
        synonymy steeped as though
            linked and unlocked,
        lest it engulf them in smoke,
                            squat,
squint-eyed god afloat in a
    saucer filled with rum.
    Steeped in memory, bedrock
        mischief, misanthropy,
                        soul
        sent rousing the dead,
                        wrested
            kiss. . .
                    Later to be
    burned, beliefless,
                        ya-habibi'd
        endlessly, burr-throat,
            threnodist. . . Lest
        it be said they saw less
            than they said, lipless,
                            less
        than a sough. . .

                    Sprocketed
    watch. Moot mechanical troth,

treadmill mesh. Ever to
be gone to again, lost
                          body
of love. . . Aspic allure,
                                lost-
limbed entanglement,
                                toxic. . .
Bitten we'd have
                          been
and were

                    •

Udhrite collapse, mute
school it advanced with. . .

Voice taken up into
airlessness, eked-out
                                insistency,
eked-out amends. . .

Strangled horse. Blistered
fist around a dove's
neck,   word brought back
from one who crossed
over,   beginning, we
                                would
say, to see the
light. . .

            In a dark room
discussing duende. Something
they saw or they thought
                                they
saw. An aura he called it,
air, though they choked on
it, smoke bound in leaves,
                          ambulant,
sleight. . .
                    Conscript air, she
replied, meaning manic,
want without remedy,
endless refrain, would

it would cease,   night
not only itself but all
nights, not-ness her
                    muse,
no light but one star, that
one star black. . .

                    Flutter spoke
    next, not flight, not
        even feeling though they
        felt it squirm its way
                        out
    from inside. . . Panicky
butterfly, lyric escape.
                    Stubbly
    cheeks' rough remembered
caress turned hunter, haunted
    her, imminent ghost, gotten
                        ready,
    resigned. . . Reminiscing the
        few for whom the word
        was enough, no longer
            among them. Never the
        same for him as for her,
                        for
them as for either, isolate,
                        again
    the awaited blow ripped
    away the wall, tore the
floorboards up

                    •

                    News
arrived as they were
    singing. Cries of thousands
    cut in on the music,
        charred bodies blown
        about, unembalmable,
                        bombed,
    these the black torsos they
        saw, no Pharaoh's
                        crypt,

                    6

night not only itself,
                    ominous
        night. . .

    No heavenly night, what
she had hoped for, later
                    crept in. . .
    Child tucked in bed while
bombs fell, ya habibi echoing
        endlessly, remedyless,
complaining *Played God,*
                    got
        burned. . .
            Burr spoke now,
    not subtly, flat sanity's
        enablement labored,
                    let go. . .
    Took between her lips their
gruff tongues' foretaste of
        "heaven," raspy word given
back by the newly
                    dead

                •

    Hummed.   "Tell me," so
disdainfully it stung. . .
                    Raw-throated
    singer beating time with a
        dry stick. . .
            Feasted on ghost-
lore, leavings, "whither thou
    goest. . ." In another house
dwelt far beyond sight. That
    they were there, anywhere
                    at all,
        ever the heist it had
always been. . .   Brute
    pointlessness bearing
                    down,
    blunt eminence. Dead the
    more alive they were
                    when

alive, less dead. "Took into
                         my hand
a straw. . ."

          Banged adamant head
      spun with plugged-in harps,
                              agitant
          oud-light,   knottedness of
      locks, disarray. . .
                    Theoretic rush, thought
          filled with blood. Dust. . . Inexistent
              water. . . Tossed rump. Rounded
          edge. Roll of the
                         earth. . .

No longer impressed, no new
      day terminus. Numbed where
   abundance led. Dazed under
      a crumbling dome,
                         torn
         socket.
                Bought soul
                         yelling
         sell
              so loud
      ears
              burned

. . . to remove the very categories of I, Thou, He, *and to become We,* such must be the meaning of the so-called "mysteries of the Simonians."

—Jacques Lacarrière, *The Gnostics*

SONG OF THE ANDOUMBOULOU: 17

— rim of the well—

Thought they were done
but it wasn't over, the
we they might've been,
would-be we. Swirl spoke, so
did whir. . . Saw the
                    he
she remembers hit by
the he she saw, witnessing
    rock to the side of his head,
                            who,
brought up short, came to, saw
    he would always be too
                    late. . .

Thought they were done, rocks
    weighed them down, thought they'd
go under. Drenched Chorus they
    called themselves, drunk,
                        maybe
        drowned,   outside, beside
themselves,   looked on. . .

                        A cold wind
    came, their teeth chattered.
Under her breath she whispered,
    "Worshippers, come
                nigh."
No longer the she they began with,
    another, not theirs,   made
of his loss a conduit,   chthonic
                        stir
    spun with

9

lapis-light

•

Rumble underfoot.
                    Train
pulling in, pulling out.
  Entrances ad infinitum,
                              exits.
  Lake they were soon to
leave made more beautiful,
    mind made to wander, what
                              follow
  what. . .

              Rough would-be love. . .
    Rough tug pulling them
        under. Having had their
  day only to have it taken
                              back. . .
    The he she remembers not
  the he she saw stepping onto
                              the train,
    ground ripped away by what
      might've been. . .

                    "Brought up
short," she blurted out before we
    could warn her whoosh was
                              afoot. . .
  A wind which wasn't a wind blew
    in, blew out. Water
  came up to their necks, we
                              thought they
  were done

              •

  So that these words rocked
    my sleep, woke me: *World in
which Hoof had its way*. . .
    He her would-be horse, she
      my would-be rider, we

                                    the
        annunciative beast at
                          well's edge. . .

    Power the problem, lack of
        power the problem. Such
        insistence meaning that much
            less the more they leaned
        on it. Not to call nemesis
                              muse
    caught what refused us,
                              spun
        one way or another, run
                          out. . .

    No quotable wisdom, whoosh
        wanted in. Wide-eyed Anuncia
        loomed in the doorway. Would-be
        statue. "Stole my heart. . ."
                              A tiny
        star stuck to the lobe of one
            ear, thread he could hang
                              from,
    wishing on it, fall if not
                          fly. . .

    Wanted to reach at the exact
        efficacious angle, the he-and-she
            of it twinned in a mirror,
                              fleet,
    inescapable two-ness fitted with
    wings, out the corner of an
                          eye. . .
    On alternate nights he threw
        sticks, lit candles, whatever
        it took. Talked at the crossroads,
            thorn in his throat.
                          "Never
    got enough to get over you. . ."
                              Heard her
        say words whoosh put in his mouth. . .

    Pocketed a rock which would be

his reminder, lidless witness,
                              wide-
      eyed stone. . . Shrunken stump hoisted
rootless, petrified light.
                         World
      hollowed out, the Andoumboulou
      beckoned. Echoed aboriginal
                              cut,
      chthonic spur

                                          Sung
                        to hammer and anvil
          accompaniment,   the rock he
                        pocketed's point song
                  painted red, Petro,
                                          eyes
                        wanting sleep
                                    rubbed raw. . .

                  Said he was obsessed,
                  made much too much
                                    of it,
                        the he she would've
                        otherwise wanted,
                                          riven
                        rock. Crawled on his
                        stomach thru dense
                                          undergrowth,
                  knocked across the head, saw
                        stars. . .
                                    "Let no tool
                  touch another," he commanded,
                                          choked
          on a kola put out for Ogun,
                  dead but for the book
                                    they
          thumbed

SONG OF THE ANDOUMBOULOU: 18

— ogou en dèz o —

Sat at the bar in the Long
Night Lounge. A cramped,
   capacious room, alternately
so, simultaneously so. . .
                      Plopped
   himself down beside me and
said, "So." Over and over
                    again said
   only, "So." Gnostic stranger
   I embraced as though it
was me I embraced. . .
                Was.
   Caught me unawares. . .

               Thus it
was these words broke my sleep,
                 woke
   me: *Heard it who seldom spoke,*
   "No remedy," flamenco's gnostic
   moan. . . Standing, I sank, felt
      nothing, though the spun words
   rocked my waking, shook me,
      spun from when body caught soul,
                     soul
body,
      "Tongue too familiar with
   tooth," I complained, blue
              Davidic
   harp, Ethiopian moan. Monophysite
      lament, one we, Ouadada, that
   we would include, not reduce to us. . .
   He to him, she to her, they to them,
                   opaque
   pronouns, "persons" whether or not we
knew who they were. . .

              Whoosh, what we
   needed, movement,   except the what-sayer,

14

obsessed, asking what. "Was it a woman
he once was in love with?" "Was it a lie
　　he'd long since put it all behind?"
　　　　　　　　　　　　　　　Not
an earring,　　inimical star the spark
she lit, burn beyond imaginable burn, "were"
　　notwithstanding,　　this what would've
been meant by bought soul. . .
　　　　　　　　　　　　Ears hot
　　with what she took to be talk not of
　　her but of someone else. Numbed
　he, numbed she, numbed we,　　numbed
affront. Feeling found in flames
　　　　　　　　　　　　　obsolete

　　　　　　　　・

　As though what they say was all we
had, that words be would, would
　　words,　　where they pointed
not beside the point though almost,
　　　　　　　　　　　　　we
　　made of how many who could say?
No we of romance we contrived
　　coupling. . . No nation's
we, collectivity's wish. . .
　　　　　　　　　　　Aberrant
　　sky, stone hoisted on stone. . .
　　Rethought what Andoumboulou
　　　　　　　　　　　　meant. . .

　Squat world,　　squat fractious
allure, failed creation,　　angels
　at the root of it, inept. Tossed
into ruins overlooking the city,
　　　　　　　　　　　　pocketed
　　rock,　　wordlike, wrestling with
sound, stir without end,　　voice
　borne up by what ailed it, dreamt
articulation, dreamt wordless
　　　　　　　　　　　rapport. . .
　　Dreamt entanglement, torn at the
　　roots. Dreamt entrenchment, not of

15

dream but inveiglement,   voice,
  thrown obliquity, bled. Sound so
                          abstruse
    we struck our heads, "Where did it
  come from?"   Point song.   Point-
      lessness.   Words wanting not to be
                              words. . .

Revelled in what once we lamented. What to
    say but that we'd been that way
  before? Every angle we'd have other-
      wise arrived by blocked,   going
    more than getting there.
                          Though
      the dense woods mocked our
      waking, rocked us, robed us
in flammable array. . .   Groped our
    way, said ready the water,
        ta'wil said to've been sown
      at the foot of a page,
                          flew
  but for the weight of Ogun's
      iron shoe,   shod ghost we
imagined we rode, running
                        in place

─────────────────

                  Seven-sided
house said to've been left
     in heaven.   Bumped affect
    only strife touches.   Strummed
harp long ago let go. . .

               Who'd
    rather wash with blood
                than with
    water they had heard, sound
    their adamant recompense, moot
    solace what solace there
                was. . .

   A martinete sung to drummed
   accompaniment. Shoulders
               bare,
  chest wrapped in cloth.
Wasted breath, wind battling
   wind, rekindling a Gypsy's
claims on Egypt. . .
          Two initiates
   locked in a cold room
             shivering.
  Remnants of an
alternate life

                                        Sound
        raveling sound calling itself
            eternity. No known locale
though names accrue. A saeta
        we heard whose head had been
                                                chipped
        from stone. Adamant ghost
inside a thick wrap of
        skin, adamant arrow.
        Remnant of an alternate
                                life. . .

        So that Ogun of Two Waters
met me in my sleep, woke
        me to my slumber, Sea of
Knowing, School of Nod. . .
                                        Two
        inebriates quibbling in a
            dimly lit room. Knife
plunged in trenchwater.
                                Stone
        hoisted on
stone

SONG OF THE ANDOUMBOULOU: 19

Notwithstanding we stood miragelike,
   outless the world he'd have
given regardless, Ahtt were it
    otherwise. "What does 'Language
    is a fruit of which the
               skin
  is called chatter' mean?" he
                  asked as we
    sat in Wrack Tavern, Inn
of Many Monikers, Long Night Lounge. . .

  Went back to the book, having
turned his back on the book,
                Cerno
Bokar musing the ruses of God. . .
  "'The flesh eloquence,'" I put
in, "'the seed good sense,'" added
  what the book went on to say.
But he dwelt on "skin," having
              sat so
  long and said only, "So," rattled
    by wisdom's visit, bits of glass
    puncturing his lips as he spoke.
    "Sophic thigh," he asserted,
              "sophic
    belly, sophic butt. . ."
          Sophic
sway he found himself taken out
  by, entranced by her impudent
  midriff,   plump lower lip,   caress
    of his neck,   calling
           him
  the apple of her eye.
         A wuh
sound sounding like dove-warble
  worked his throat, the we
he, she and I were haunted by.
  An ur-sound blew thru our
         bones,

muted kanoun run, heat from
a blistered sun. . .

                    Blue Sufi
lounge where the brethren met,
                            Wrack
        Tavern. . . Sat sipping Sidi
        Brahim. . . Hsissen hit a note no
        one knew existed, the song had
                            begun,
        song said to be of the Andoumboulou,
            as if Ogo, Gnaoua-like, had gone
            north,   gnostic reminder of
        world-rut,   remnant,   revenant,
                whirled,   unraveling,   whir. . .
Words bandaging wind, self-styled
        imperium, albeit all who'd have
        seen it so withdrew. "I'm the last
        bird to leave before the storm,"
                            she
        announced. "Thought bread was a new
            kind of cloth. I'm the Bedouin
            hick you've heard about. . ." Asked her
            name, she answered, "Sophia,"
                            arrived
        at his door that day, hair streaked
        with henna,   in whose dream he was an
            accordion-player in Algiers,   a
        trick played by the mind, he said,
    uninevitable she. . .

                    Uninevitable they,
        however much it seemed otherwise,
                            that
        they were there, that events had
        brought them to this, notwithstanding
        she stood oasislike, sway of
                            palms
        and of hips, her adamance notwithstanding. . .
    "Mud cooled our feet," he told her, words
        to a song he'd have given the world
        to hear her sing,   uninevitable
                            he,

20

who, asked his name, gave only his
middle, "Music,"   mask made of
     wind, of wrack,   by which if
by wind it meant soul it meant
                              salvage

SONG OF THE ANDOUMBOULOU: 20

I was the what-sayer.
Whatever he said I would
   say so what.
             Boated whether
we came by train or by
   bus,   green light
loomed on the horizon.
   Where we were might've
been the moon. . .

             Bleak
  survival egged us on, a
   bird made of tin
   pressing its beak
     to the smalls of our
   backs. Spectral
           advance,
  peripatetic
        spur. . .
This while on our
  way to Ouadada,
            vowed we'd
  let nobody turn us
   around, thought we
  saw Dadaoua. To the outer
    principalities of Onem we were
   brought,   bought,
              sold
on blocks, auctioned
          off.

It was a train we were on,
  peripatetic tavern we
were in, mind unremittingly
  elsewhere, words meaning
              more
   than the world they
  pointed at,   asymptotic
    tangent,   Atht it

was called. . .
                    Sophic rail we
          stood at listening.
                              Expression
          was on the jukebox, "To Be."
          Spooked flutes hollowed
                                        us out,
             sophic not-ness. . . South, more
          news of slaughter. Something
       we saw we hoped we only
             imagined we saw. "They
                                   kill us,"
Mbizo yelled. . .

                         Sat on a
          train crossing adverse
          heaven. Raz they called
          it, fractured masses. . .
                              Arz it
             could've easily been, more
                  likely Zra,   Zar the
             asymptotic arrival we
                                    glimpsed,
             "Not yet" yelled at every
                                    stop.
Stone rail. Stone climb. Stone
          motion. . . "Beast in kin's
       clothing," someone said, went on
       about Ciskei. Someone
       punched "People Get Ready"
          on the jukebox, Spear's
                              ash
             anointment lumped our
                  throats. . . Went to speak
             but only dust came out.
                    Went to run but what was
          now most real was the "away
                                   from."
       Horns blew to woo the unready,
                                   not
             answering when it would
       be Ouadada

———————

Wondered would we ever
surface. "Not yet,"
    the conductor yelled
at every stop.
                Wondered
was it even a train we were
    on, if it was was it
    going the right way.
                    Dreamt
        it was a plane we were on, as if
        it was an in-flight
                        movie. . .
        On the screen two pairs of lips
                                met,
            some incumbent taste caught
                in their mouths for
        years finally kissed
                    away,

    a way of holding the world at
        bay, out of reach, not to
    know what they'd missed when it
            was gone. . .
                    Likewise we
        the collective kiss we
            called Ouadada. Leapt
                        across
        unwon space, pure
    caprice

•

He who'd have said
we so assured it
  was a plain we
were on, flat for as
far as the eye
        could see
    around him, Raz
with an *e* on the
end. A way of
spelling, a spell if
  by *e* we meant
       exit,
          trackless
the train we rode, so
  abruptly conductorless,
riderless, ghost
      of what it
  was,   an awayness
receding as fast as
  he approached,
        gone
  could he have
       gotten
there. . .
     Into the
shed, might wood
  be water, sophic
skirt with him under
    it as if it was a
  tent, pitched as
       would a
  note be, only were wood
        water,
 rasp our lone
    resort

A red, yellow and
green scroll standing watch
over the city,
proclamations
wet on every lip
as we disembarked,

those
who had been before
and those the newly
risen,
would-be abjuration
swirled away. . .

Noses
wide with the smell of
earth after rain,
held each other,
lifted,
let go

We who will have been
compost could wood be
                          water,
     world a burning hut,
     white wreck less of
        ship than of
                     solace, phosphorus
     dropped in water,   caw,
        lipped conduit,
                       razed
     had we had our
way

•

    He said he would say
nothing. I whatever
  popped into my
              head.
  We knew there was
a world somewhere.
                How to get
  there no, would we get
                  there no. . .
He said, not knowing that,
    he would say
    nothing. I,
          him having
  popped into my head,
              said
  the same

Rift we called
Qareeb, asymptotic
    nearness, ana-
    grammatic Star. . .
A way of holding the
world at bay. Less
    to look than get a
    glimpse in passing. . .
                        Qareeb
    we called it, calling in
    vain. Rast, anagrammatic
                    Tsar. . .
        No such we the where
            we knew. Pres's
        "people" an illusion
            music said was
            no illusion. Ruse
            it behooved us beware
                of. Agitant oud-string,
                Abdel Salim's octet. . .
        Sudan it seemed it was
                we rode thru,
                        there
        nowhere and where we
                        were

SONG OF THE ANDOUMBOULOU: 21

Next a Brazilian cut came
on Sophia picked. Paulinho's
  voice lit our way for what
    seemed eternity,
                minha
    primeira vez the one
                  phrase
  we caught or could understand,
    no matter it ended
soon as it'd begun.
                Endless
  beginning. Endless goodbye.
    Always there if not ever all
there, staggered collapse, an
    accordion choir serenaded
                  us,
  loquat groves hurried by
    outside. . .

          It was a train
  in southern Spain we
    were on, notwithstanding
    Paulinho's "first" put one
      place atop another,
              brought
    Brazil in, air as much of
it as earth, even more, an ear
    we'd have called inner unexpectedly
    out. . . Neither all in our
heads nor was the world an array
                  less
  random than we'd have
          thought. . .
It was a train outside São
  Paulo on our way to Algeciras we
  were on. . . Djbai came aboard.
  Bittabai followed. . .
           A train
  less of thought than of quantum

solace, quantum locale. "Quantum
   strick, bend our way," we
begged, borne on by reflex, a
                          train
   gotten on in Miami, long since
gone

                 •

   Lag was our true monument.
   It was an apse we strode under,
       made of air. There inasmuch
as we exacted it, aliquant amble,
                               crowds
   milling around on corners began
   to move, the great arrival day
       we'd heard so much about begun,
sown even if only dug up again.

   Call it loco, lock-kneed samba. . .
Multi-track train. Disenchanted
   feet. . .
           It was the book of
it sometimes going the wrong
   way we now read and wrote. . .
                              Split
   script. Polyrhythmic
remit

SONG OF THE ANDOUMBOULOU: 22

Took me aside with more talk of
Sophia.　　Hot summer stillness.
　　Hieratic stir.　　Press of her
　　　hips beneath a loose cotton
　　　　　　　　　　　　　dress,
　　　bright sun behind her. Graspable
　　　waist, sinewy limbs, see-thru
　　　　　　　　　　　　　cloth. . .
　　Climbed a ladder he said she climbed
　　　ahead of him, looked up her
dress. Saw planets, furtive hair,
　　　the insides of her thighs. . .
　　　　　　　　　　　　Sometimes
　　　called it a tree, sometimes called
　　it a ladder. Stroked his chin, stood
　　　recounting the lift of it, the
　　　we they became to hold on to it,
　　　　　　　　　　　　　fraught
limbs having so to do with sun
　　　it seemed it flew. "Some ride it
　　　sounds like" was all I could
　　　　　　　　　　　　say. . .

　　Sometimes called it a tree,
　　sometimes called it a ladder. Vague,
　　　sometimes not so vague hunger
for what wasn't there. . . Announced
　　he wanted only what's hidden,
　　　　　　　　　　　　　kept
　　　hidden, but she too took me
　　　aside. . . Called it a tree, also
　　　called it her "clime,"
　　　　　　　　　　　　the
　　tree they left the train
　　　　　　　　　　　to pick
fruit from. . .　　Knew he'd be
　　looking, she said, gave him an
　　eyeful. Pulled itself up out
of the ground, began to shake,

32

                                        fruit
        falling as they too would've
    done had they not held on,
                                        a tree
        they got off the train to pick
                                        loquats
    from. . .
                    Knew she knew that he would
        be watching, he said. *More-than-
        meets-the-eye* notwithstanding,
                                        looked
        his fill. *No-sooner-had-she-told-him-
        not-to* notwithstanding, regardless he
        knew already what he'd see. . .

                                        Woven of
    sun, sun woven of cloth inflaming their
        bodies, a glimpse he said she gave
        him into what lay beyond the grave.
                                        "Some
        ride it sounds like" was all I could
                                        say. . .
    Taken aside, I stood immune to their talk,
        kept to one side of it, notwithstanding I'd
        have wished otherwise. Reft eloquence
        had hold of their throats but kept
                                        me at
    arm's length,   shower said to have
        been of secret things utterly suspect,
        lift said to have been of a loquat
        tree. . . Took him in under limbs
                                        filled
    with multi-seeded fruit, more seed than
                                        fruit,
        meat so much less than sense were
        seed sense, bone might be seed,
                                        she
    said

●

What elsewhere loomed under
branches and leaves and a
   billowing dress. . . Now sat
saying nothing, working a pepper
seed caught in his teeth. . .
                 How to
   say he'd seen, how he'd ever
sing it,   voice bottom-heavy
   but nonetheless float,   an
                    aloof,
   light-bodied bigness, something
                    he saw,
    said he saw, unable to quite
say what he saw. . .

              Rude epiphany,
dreamt or pretended,   that there
   be the illusion something lay
in back, loomed above, ubiquitous
   book, wrought leafless wood. . .
                  Swung
book. "Ythmic sway," he begged,
               "be
   with me," a new recruit
into Ogun's unruly way. . .

   Played flute in the shade of a
tree she called her woodshed.
  Book of anabatic limbs,
  bruited wing-stir. Fell
             for the
  look of the child in him,
he for the same in her.
            Gnostic remains
of what, come into the world, she
  relinquished,   wed short of
wood becoming water, wrought wood out
               of water,
 would they were
there again

Apocryphal book of the loquat
tree. Uninevitable she of the ripe
lower lip. Impudent pout upon
impudent pout, promiscuous
                              mouthsmear,
        rash, uninevitable kiss. . .

What had been a train was now a
        bus between Fez and Tetuan,
                                    Ahttless
        mountains viewed from in front of
Brain Lake. . .
                Loquat exuberance
got the best of them, loquat
        eloquence, loquat allure.
                                This
they admitted later out loud in
        their sleep. As if to say soul
seeks out low places. . . As if
        to say loquat height let go,

                                rotting
        fruit lay at the foot of the
tree, having gone to their heads.
        Loquat elixir. Ambient wine.
                                Ubiq-
        uitous whiff

SONG OF THE ANDOUMBOULOU: 23

— rail band—

Another cut was on
the box as we pulled
  in. Fall back though we
did once it ended,
              "Wings
  of a Dove" sung so
  sweetly we flew. . .
The Station Hotel came
into view. We were in
  Bamako. The same scene
  glimpsed again and
    again said to be a
            sign. . .
As of a life sought
  beyond the letter,
  preached of among those
who knew nothing but,
           at yet
  another "Not yet" Cerno
    Bokar came aboard, the
  elevens and the twelves locked
    in jihad at each other's
throats,   bracketed light
  lately revealed, otherwise
           out. . .
Eleven men covered with
mud he said he saw. A
  pond filled with water
white as milk. Three chanting
  clouds that were crowds of
  winged men and behind the
           third
  a veiled rider, Shaykh
        Hamallah. . .

For this put under house arrest
  the atavistic band at the
station reminded us, mediumistic

                        squall we'd have maybe made
                                        good on
        had the rails we rode been
                                Ogun's. . .
            Souls in motion, conducive
            to motion,   too loosely
            connected to be called a
            band, yet "if souls converse"
        vowed results from a dusty
                                        record
        ages old

                        •

            Toothed chorus. Tight-jawed
        singer. . .   Sophic strain,
            strewn voice, sophic stretch. . .
        Cerno Bokar came aboard,
                                        called
                war the male ruse,
                                        muttered
            it under his breath, made sure
                                        all within
                earshot heard. . .
                                Not that the
                hoarse Nyamakala flutes were
        not enough, not that enough
            meant something exact
                                        anymore. . .
            Bled by the effort but sang
                even so,   Keita's voice,
                                        Kante's
        voice, boast and belittlement
            tossed back and forth. . .
                                        Gassire's
            lute was Djelimady Tounkara's
                                        guitar,
        Soundiata, Soumagoro, at each other's
            throat. . .   Tenuous Kin we called
        our would-be band, Atthic Ensemble,
                                        run
            with as if it was a mistake we made
        good on,   gone soon as we'd

                        37

gotten
there

·

Neither having gone nor not having
   gone, hovered,   book, if it
                           was a
book, thought wicked with wing-stir,
     imminent sting. . . It was the book
  of having once been there we
     thumbed, all wish to go back
     let go,   the what-sayer,
                      farther
     north, insisting a story lay
  behind the story he complained he
     couldn't begin to infer. . .
                   What
  made him think there was one
  we wondered, albeit our what
 almost immediately dissolved as we
                      came
  to a tunnel, the train we took
ourselves to be on gone up in
    smoke,   people ever about to get
ready, unready, run between what,
                  not-what.
    And were there one its name was
  Ever After, a story not behind but in
    front of where this was,   obstinate
  "were," were obstinate so susceptible,
                  thin
  etic itch, inextricable
         demur

·

  Beginningless book thought to've
unrolled endlessly, more scroll
  than book, talismanic strum.
As if all want were in his holding
    a note   only a half-beat
             longer,

another he was now calling love
a big rope, sing less what
he did than sihg, anagrammic sigh,
from *war the male ruse* to *"were" the
new ruse,* the what-sayer,
sophic
stir. . . Sophic slide of a cloud across
tangency, torque, no book of a
wished else the where
we
thumbed

SONG OF THE ANDOUMBOULOU: 24

Had gotten off the bus to
pee in a field on the side
  of the road, the women
                  farther
   in than the men, the low
  hems of their dresses held
  up, hips all but touching
  the ground. . .
              So it was
  I took it they meant low
squat, loquat was code.
  Something, heads tilted
               birdlike,
  we heard, beaks what before
  had been lips. The world's
raw want, could it all have
    been so compressed. . .
                Land
  late of one whom love set
             wandering. . .
Thin peninsular reef, abstract
              earth. . .
  Took between his lips her
cusp of tongue's foretaste
  of "heaven,"   ravenous
            word they
  heard urging them on, loquat
  spin. Teeth broke biting
  her lip,   intoxicant meat he'd
              been
  warned against, took between
  his teeth. . . Took between
  his own her bleeding lip's
           lost
  lustre,   ravenous
          word
  taken back, bitten into,
         burst. . .

Whereupon the what-sayer
                              stepped
          in and said something,
          what plot there was one of
          stepping on, stepping
                              off,
               entrances more than
               remembered, exits, djinns
               making off with what where
                              we had
     left,   the slow toll it
                              took,
          low grumbling of drums. . .
     What we they exacted spread as
myth insisted, so that we for
          whom the word was long dead
                              said so
     be it, that on such-and-such a
     day So-and-So woke up to
                              a new
          life,   rid of wish, moot
          would-it-were-so, moot
                              remorse,
          out no less a part of it
               than in, in out,
               such the one place they
                              might meet,
     mute School-of-What-Hurts
                              her
          husk of a voice
revive
          them in

41

●

Push come to shove she'd
be with him he thought,
    push came to shove.
Raz was the city in
                    ruins
    they ran away from,
    legs bent ready to
        spring, hellbent on
                    heaven,
    lit between themselves a
star.
        Rubbed, made war on
"were," stayed within,
    caught in a flame she'd
have warned was coming,
        The low wrath of Dadaoua
    painted on a wall,
                    thin
        scribbling thick with
    what depth he read into it,
                        sat
        sipping hemlock it seemed. . .

    Another beating. Business-as-usual.
        Chapter 8,281,404. . .
                        A tale
    too inane to be told, she'd
        say, "say" so unequal
    to the task she'd sing, a
sound so to the side of enoughness,
    a night in Tunisia, a
                    chicken
        with lips. . .

                    Had it been
    he she advised he'd have
        ignored it. That it
    was something he'd overheard
        hit home. . . Irritant
    "say" so abrasive its rasp
                    took up

              asking what but an unintended
                  sign would get it said. . .
                                      This
          in a place named No-Such-Place,
                                          burred
              speech of a ghost named
          Not-All-There

Asked had he been hit he
answered yes. Ouab'da he
    called it as if it was a
        place,   made-up name he
    made mean "beat with clubs,
                                kicked,"
        what as-if there was long
        since fallen away. It was
        a place brought boots
    to the ribs, batons to the
                                back. . .
    Ouab'da he called it, said it
was a place, knew, if not already,
        he'd be hit. . .
                    Split lift,
            sat ravished, over-
                taken, overwhelmed. . .
                                Ouab'da
        he named it, said it was a
                                place,
            never to go back
        there again

SONG OF THE ANDOUMBOULOU: 25

—"zar" nth part—

Throughout it all a buzzing
   drum at our backs. Again
  it was a train we were on.
Outside the window came a sign
  read "Ouar," we scratched our
                heads.
No such place on the schedule we
  read, no such where. . . Why no
  "Not yet" yelled now we shouted
    out, doubting what good it
              would do. . .
Saw Ouagadou, sought Ouadada. No
point protesting warned a mouth
  made of catfish teeth. . .
             Chanted
Where is your love, chanted *Run,*
  come, rally, chanted *What, blood,*
  put it in place, pull it
           apart,
  chanted *Chant down Babylon*. . .
On its rise we the dismembered
winced. Inasmuch as what we want
  was unreal there it stood, "four
  times fallen asleep" not even
            close,
  came to where they'd always been.
               Bombed
  origins, splendorless, war their
one resolve. Reich without end its
  aim, omnibus hitlist. . .
          Hurtless.
            Unctuous.
Oiled. . .

    Tarred birds' wings. End-of-the-
world augury, new world omen. . .
  First blood sweet to the tongue,
  bitter going down. Tenuous. Ouagadou D.C.

45

Mothered in blood, on blood

               gotten

big beyond limit. Said of its
demise we welcomed it, whispering
limit's will be done

           even so. . .

                  Heard

my head say cradle me, myself cradle
my head. Wondered whose head I meant,
what voice I spoke with, volitionless,

                 feet

stuck to the floor. . .

          A balloon tore

loose, floated off, I called it
back. . . B'Head looked in from

             on high. . .

Said a bomb fell on its foot, said
B'Dot, said killing floor. Better
to be somewhere else we thought,

            called

elsewhere Mozambique, Might've-Been. . .

               B'Legless.

Last resort. . .

        Adamant muses in lewd

array, thin trumpeter's lips against
the mouthpiece pressed against angular
exit, glimpse of a ghost,   gaze a

            ghost

would give,   hushed if not harbored,

              hummed. . .

Was it a place we wondered, my head spun,
bodiless, hit by nobody knew what. . .
Beneath crosshairs hoisted in green
light, earth of Hurqalya, obstinate,
caught. . .   Genetic letter, inaccessible

              alphabet. . .

Begged of the moment be my Imam. . .
Lost cause the lore you lament he
announced, said of the Udhrite

             school

soy la ley, said say tonu soy. . .

Was it a place we wondered, balloonless,
        bewildered. Hollow be my name I grumped. . .
    Arab strings made us neigh like
        horses. Atavist run, pa'l monte,
    mounted, adamant heads made of
                            heartbreak
brass

II

STRA

SONG OF THE ANDOUMBOULOU: 26

— stra precipice —

Something like a valley it
was we came to next. Collapsed
  aura long thirsted after,
  looked at from afar, faded,
                   fell
    away once we arrived,
                 evanescent
Stra. . .   Cloudbank. Low-swung
  sky. Love's low estate. . .
"Ra's was the world, Raz what was
  made of it." This he muttered
                under
    his breath again and again. Had
    suffered a great blow one
              sensed. . .

Great gaping wound. All nod, all
knowing. Maybe had a gun put to
  the back of his head, cold air
blow thru. Had suffered a great
              blow
    he called C'rib. . . Had had a
    pistol put to the back of
    his head or might as well
           have,
died, came back to life under
  loquat leaves. . . Hoisted cloth
conjured falling water, consecrated
    to those "who heard guns of
    war." Distant horns droned,
             dressed
us in mud, spewed out remonstrances. . .
  Flutes filled our heads from
before I was born. . .

          The drum whose
voice buzzed he made a watery
  altar, "ultimate" altar: champagne,

white roses, green grapes. Cried
    cracked ribs rolled him in mud,
                              marrow
made him weep. "Cracked ribs rolled me
    in mud," he kept repeating. C'ahtt
    was the web she wore, wound him
                              up in,
      C'rib her sophic sway, tossed hips.
    So that these words walked our sleep,
        roused us: *Edge be my birthright,*
chipped, broken off, jag what where
                              soever. . .
    Atthic stragglers we knew ourselves to
        be, so-called caught up. C'rib's
    catered ache embraced us, asymptotic
ambush,   lag,   nastic
                      rush

Arrived late in a land known as
Nudge. There was a ledge we stood
on, leaned over, looked down.
                                    "Bone
be our bridge," we begged, "vertiginous
        brink. . ." Jaws drawn heavenward
creaked, rickety wood, abrupt
        mandibular strick. . .
                                    Thin
    skin of the earth were it
stilts we stood on.
    Thin thread undoing the
rags we wore. . . The word *arrival*
    stuck to my lip, hung
                        down
    like a cigarette. . .
    Home.   Harbor.   Hush. . .
                            Gone up
in smoke

•

What had been a buzz became the
ocean's roar, Lone Coast the entropic
shore it washed us up on, Zar
the utopic city built on sand. . .

                             Again
he and she took me aside, asymptotic
twins, the we they intimated,
hinted at, heard had been lost,
equal each to another, slightly

                            askew. . .
Rebegan the book of having once been
there, now by default. . . Book of
having been there once he now called
it, mind, one heard it said, in the
gutter, intimating the gutter

                         ran
under her dress. . . Deciduous cloth
subtly tugged, unraveling. Late
lore, what of which he remembered made
him weep. C'rib the consoling sway
unconsoling, words' errant air

                          run out
into air. . . Distant kin called after
as if they'd eventually return,
prodigal soul albeit soul so named it,
pent, profligate lip, uninterpretable
tongue. . .

             Profligate beat. Veiled bone.
Splayed samba. Head long pitted
with voices, nonchalant. Something
stood inside, stepped forward, said,

                         "So."
Again said, over and over, only,
"So." Albeit history stacked high on its
back made other claims. . . Cavernous
book. Long talk. Taken land. . .

                         That
it be the book of believing they
had no book, memory dead but for
one recollection, stripped limbs

                              catching
late October
          light

Nastic swell.   Gnostic dispatch.
Stripped limbs would be arms and
    legs were wood water, mixed
metamorphic flow. Leafless
                              book,
        blank watery pages,
                              there
            to be written on if he
                          could. . .
Champagne would be sea-foam,
    green grapes nominal white,
white roses mean what white
    roses mean, this the
                    what-sayer's
        ta'wil. . . They would be we,
                              twinless,
        bane he bore witness to.
Grain of sand and of salt
    mechanical twinship
    overlooked. . . Gremlin.
                          Luddite
        ghost

·

We were in retreat,   beginning to
bid the senses goodbye, not yet
     ready,   wondering if we'd ever
be and if ever when,   walked a
     deserted beach on Lone Coast. . .
                                   There

     was a shell they held to my ear,
hollow head at last emptied of
expectation, profligate host,
                              tart

     fruit tasting of salt, the sea
nearby. . .   Listened against my
     will it turned out, broke what I
took to be code under Steal-Away Ridge,
                                    earth

     lately compounded of wistfulness,
wish,   tart fruit tasting of sand. . .
Loquat Cove meant loquat close,
meaning he'd have been closer than
     the tights beneath her dress
     had he had his way, the rain he
        saw soaking her skin under heavy
     cloth   a cutaneous tide, fraught,
                                  wavelike

     spray, Sufic nearness, wool worn
well into summer, Sufic sweat,
                              she
     too tending that way, fraught, salty
ta'wil intimated under black, tightfitting
                                  cloth. . .

     Clouds broke, lightning lit the sand on Lone
        Coast. Wet, they scurried for shelter,
found it, later named it Loquat Cove.
     This they said into my ear, spoke
     in unison, each the other's Lone
                                  Coast

     alibi, patterless feet wiping away
        what earth was left. . . Bent on
     release, bent on being trackless,
soul so repeatedly said to abide shipwreck,

57

                wanted it, wooed it, won. . .
                                        This
        they whispered into my ear, I was
          wide awake. . . Sought rise loquat was
        code for, low squat's logarithmic
                                        ladder,
            exponential ambush, exponential
          debris. . . Were there the place they'd
            have held it, thin peninsular wisp,
        swayed by the feel of rain on the backs
              of their necks,   precipitous,
            peripatetic Stra. . . Stray precipice,
                                        ledged
            air beckoned, what I wouldn't
          hear relegated to waves' edge,
                                retold
        on low-toned flutes. . .
                            Came then
          to the land of low branches,   stooped
        as we made our way, wind warmed our
            necks. Book drawn in flammable ink,
          redacted leaflight. Bare skin scratched
              by dry underbrush. . . "Lost"
                                        book
        of under, book of
                            undone

Went now by two new names,
Hummed Outer Meat, Hollowness,
   these the he and she
              whose
tale the shell rehearsed,
    we were they otherwise.
                      Banged
   our heads, stricken wall we
      called Yonder,   abstract
body we took ourselves to be. . .
    Called it a meeting, a
                    melding point,
    they insisted. Melting, we
   insisted back. . .

             Stitched lips
   spoke of parting,   not
much to say but that they
   told one so.
          Something
so-called spoke from
   a horizontal slit cut
under their noses,
            each the
   other's non-pronominal
                 elsewhere,
   nominal
 out

59

We were running,   I away
   from Loquat Cove, those two
                        toward it.
      Cracked bone spoke, called us
its envoy,   bade us bid sense
      goodbye, so scarce it was. . .
   Both spoke, he and she, insistent,
      he that wisdom came from the
   sky in the shape of a woman,
                              she
      that it came from the ground
         in the shape of a man. . .
                              A quake
   shook the sand, stopped us. The earth
      moved as if we stood on stilts.
   Breath was all either wore, cracked
                              bone
their ornaments. Cracked bone spoke,
                              whistling
      fissure. . . Bumped,
         shaken frame
      sang bass

Stranded amalgam,   Saint
Anger she called it. There
  as though it hovered above,
                    off
    to one side of her, rush
      becoming one with nemesis,
    nastic remit made reticular,
     intricately amiss, rare
andoumboulouous "it."
                  Was it a
    he, was it a she, should
    it matter, she wondered,
                answered
    whether it should it did,
  called it a he. . . Could
    even feel the grain of his
  back,   whose hips would
    be hers were she her own to
                remake. . .

  Wondered why she was there
   with him again, doubly
there albeit twinless,
             entwined,
    might've been him imagining
   her in his place. The he-and-she
   she wanted, the he-and-she
they were,   rift was the
             valley
    they mapped, met in again,
     no matter she'd have
    moved on had she had her way. . .
So far from him finding reminders of
      him. . . Haunted by the
    would-be, the wasn't,
             wanting
    it so, ribcage pressed
  against ribcage, begged, "Edge
    be inductive cut, adage,

bone be egress, out."
Lay on
her back looking up at the
sky, sand a reflector
of light she dreamt he lay
on, lit sand's exhibit,
bones
underneath, agitant, exed-out
skin. . . Twinning spin put on
it, andoumboulouous prod, omen,
imprint.
Abrupt x-ray strand, andoumboulouous
bolt. . .

As if their struck limbs never
recovered, rise with its bite
fallen from them though they did,
deep indigenous cut, plangent
recess. . .
Twin ship long stranded above said
to be the soul's boat, ship
he lay on whose deck looking down
from, boated-away kin looking
back. . .

Thin strip of beach known as
He-and-She Strand, a stone's
throw, they say, from Loquat
Cove, also known as Nudge,
pocketed rock's utmost reach
might
wood be water. . .

Abject address,
abject appointment kept.
Runaway clan C'rib's
careless
law

·

Dreamt of her mother
a dream of Lone Coast.
Thin line blurring
truth, open trespass.
                          Told
    her he was already
    dead, long since
        gone,   taunted
her she didn't even know.
        Awoke from it unable to
    sleep, wanting to sleep,
        wanting to take back
                          what she
        said. . .
                The she she
    might've been lay beside him
        counting, there though
there was nothing of
    number, consequence,
                          Iemanjá
        the mother she
        mourned momentarily
            bone-close, sweet
        sleep shaken with
                          salt. . .
    Roll of waves, green
        grapes the color
    of ghost eyes,
                          gray,
wind-stricken
    scree. . . Stark
    sun the afternoon
        she accepted
                          it. . .
    Wound she would
    return to endlessly. . .
    Cut string caroling
                          world
relapse

63

●

Outside the
train the world
    ran by, fugitive
  landscape many
                    mistook,
     took to be Skid. . .
  C'rib called
out to while she
  slept, thick
  scent of cigar
                    smoke
    the pillow still
    smelled of,
                    apostrophic
    "mu" more related
    to miss than to myth,
                              hers
    had he only
  been there

SONG OF THE ANDOUMBOULOU: 28

Runaway bus I dreamt we rode
in dreaming. Traveling tavern
  I lay on my side inside.
  Muttering, "Snowbank be my
                              pillow,"
    wondering what it was
    we wanted only accident
    addressed. . . Bus hit an icy
curve, slid off the road,
      slid a split-second short
    of Ever After, rested on
                         a bed
    of snow. . .

              Where we were
    was no Namoratunga. No
African stonehenge halted our
    skid. It was the book of
                    infinitesimal
        rescue we thumbed, fraught, flat
                                   page,
      glimmering world-rut. . .
    Sleet sheet of outfulness,
      awayfulness,   numb,
                         long-
    fisted stir. . .

               A balloon lay
    beside me, breath I couldn't
    catch. Up thru an open
                      window
it went.   Faro's boat. Pharoah's
                             boat.
      Faro's, Pharoah's
                    both. . .
    A new cut now on the box
instructed us. . . Apostrophic
    bus, antientropic we,
                       B'Us

65

we called it. Djbai had come
                              aboard,
        Bittabai followed. The balloon
        lay disguised as a child. . .
        The new cut now on the box
        was "Capricorn Rising." A chain
                                came
        down, yanked us out of it.
        Runaway B'Us we hit
                        Saturn's
            rings in it seemed,
        spun, split-scripted
            skid. . . An abrupt chain
        pulled us out of our orbit.
                        Never
            a less likely place to be,
                            tangential
            advent. Grab-obsessed. Avid.
        Adamant none was ever
                        not

•

We were the world   careening
off-course, out of control.
    A second, third, fourth, nth
    wind blew thru our exhaustion,
                     blackened
     what snow pillowed our
               skid. . .

Another cut now on the box
held us up, endless hovering,
   "Afro-Blue," Trane's
   Birdland date. . . Endless
                 release,
    endless last half-minute,
               winded
    flutter. Felt for the floor,
     felt it wasn't there.
   We were the book, the
    buried page, the anomalous
bed of snow,   swung polity
                 auditing
   abject edge, agitant straw, tossed
                out of
   ourselves, taken back.

We were the dead, some
  deciduous grief the
ground we slid on.
            Something
   new now on the box we
   hadn't heard before,
             unsuspected
    advent, *Live at the Wander
    Inn* we read. . .
          We were
   the dead's fey wish to
     return,   fish reeled
   in prematurely tossed back,
            script
    hastily written hurriedly
   erased

Believed we had risen
above, buried in snow.
    Cold comfort what desperate
solace,   anagrammatic
        sub, anagrammatic
                        bus,
        andoumboulouous
                        B'Us.
    Tricks played with letters,
                            little
        else. . .

            White book, numb
    fingers. Could barely turn
                    the page. . .
        Wet book had we arrived in
    Ttha, stuck pages. One
way or the other
                unread

He spoke in tongues, for a
time at least. Spoke in
tongues until tongues' lipped
itch exhausted us.
                    C'rib
whispered into one ear,
    Crash commandeered the
                              other. . .
    Crushed fruit underfoot as
if again to begin again, what
    before so spoke to ritual
                              relent,
        begged it be otherwise. . .

Perfume falling from her
    dress, the heady press of
it, reft highness underneath.
    Had its hem draped his
                              neck, he
        dreamt, head wrapped in
    cloth made the world go
                              away. . .
    He her peepshow hostage, she
        his loquat host, this their
what-if but real, wanting more,
        world made more real, maybe
                              not, not
knowing which,   fruit found on a bed
    of snow. . .
                    Anomalous bed they
    called "loquacious,"   melodious
        word whose root they mistook,
                              took
        to mean loquat-sweet. . .
                              Obsessed
    with meaning, made its meaning,
        precocious wind, aromatic sky. Loin
    musk, loquat scent, sexed index of
        underness thickening the air

though the air grow thinner the
                              higher
            they climb. . . Curve of the earth
        as if to have already left, thrown
            world-rump,   hurt-mouth reminder,
        bruised fruit. . . Loquat curve, "loquacious"
        bend, putative pillow talk. . .
                              Ramp. . .
Would-be release. . .

                        Translated Hendrix
            into Moroccan slang, said he
            once met the Devil on a train
        outside Milan. *This the way it
                              was told
            to me,* I woke up remembering, the
                                          train
            filling up so rapidly, he said,
        the world wanted in it
                        seemed

                    •

        C'rash it became, he said next.
C'rib went on putting its
        tongue to what ears would listen.
        B'Us was the craft we rode,
        it kept assuring us, name
                        not even
            we could arrest. . .
                        Abject we
        given sibling spin, B'Us took
            every curve without even a skid,
                              C'rib
        assured us, rocked us ever so gently,
            bordered on sleep. . .

                        Crash
could be no more intact than
                              C'rib,
        C'rash reminded us. A crack
        ran thru it. Thru it we
                        made our
escape

．

It was a boat whatever it was
we were on were wood water,
   world a diluvian rut. Pocked
earth, remote feather,
                  face,
   additive altar. . . "World be
wet where we boat," he begged,
Ra's were it his to name. . .
                   That the
   spirit move thru cloth was
his wish, flag lift her liftedness
higher, offered cloth, arrowhead
under his pillow the night before,
                    leaf
   laid in the fork of a tree. . .
                She
   visited him, he visited me, I
     visited them. "She was my leaf
   laid in the fork of a tree,"
he part said, part sang, nose
              bled
   by qu'ahttet height. Cut scrub
               around
the trunk of a mubo tree brought to
   mind by her dress, limbed epiphany
I passed on as hearsay, abrupt
   visitor going on about
               "light
glimpsed underneath," claiming
              to be me,
strange kin. . . Medicinal sweat wet the
   arrow he slept with, a saeta he heard
at a distance, faint, ghost of his
   whatsaid self, dead already,
called himself "so-called me". . .

Off to the side of what altered
the closer we came to it, there
   the less there we were. . .
              Came to
the land of the newly tongued,

                                        having what
    to say but that before they had
    no voice we ended up asking,
                                        wood
        battling wood wood's release,
                                        that it
    be water, cloth to caught wind's dry
                                        wood

                        •

    Long night in which the ripped,
    archetypal two took me aside. . .
    Saw bones where before there
    were branches, eyes bunched
                                        into an
        x-ray squint. . . Nothing, not
    a stitch underneath he said
                                        she wore,
            beside himself, talked all out
    of his head. Pitiless thought
        known as "meant to be" meant
    "wanted it so," world repossessed,
                                        risen,
    rebegun, wed only if wood became
    water. . .

            More he than himself,
    non-pronominal scat we now
                                        sang,
        more than he could say we saw. . .
                                        B'Us
    was our boat, our sub should
        we go under, he her loquat hostage,
                                        she
        his gnostic
    twin

B'Us was code for buzz. Buzz
was also code. . . Taken aside,
  for a time at least, we spoke as
one. We were three. The spirit
                          being with
      us made us four. We now called
  ourselves a qu'ahttet, Sophia's
        coinage. His was her mouth,
    my mouth, its mouth, no longer
      andoumboulouous, one. . .

                          Out of
        our heads the more out of our
                          heads it
      seemed to have come.
                    Qu'ahttet, double
      qu'ahttet, quadruple qu'ahttet, ad
    infinitum. Qu'ahttet was our whatsaid
      writ, stropped wish, sky rubbed
                          earthward,
      raw

•

We were now somewhere whose
name was Nonsonance,   voiceless
   the word whose adumbration
bound our book,   booked
      blood wood's admonition,
                              trickling
      wood played on by mallets,
balafonic bridge we crossed over
      on. Nonsonant wood laid like
   railroad ties, planked insistence. . .
   Ribbed water made "were"
                        to itself. . .

On the edge of an "it" otherwise
   out of reach we disembarked,
rim of no well we'd ever
   drink from,   asymptotic
water,   hyperbolic thirst. . .
      Where we were slowly lulled us
   to sleep. Music from the year I was
      born leapt off the box, Bird's
Benzedrine reed woke us up.
                        Too late
      for that, nonsonant wood
   announced, said without sound.
      Lacktone said it best.
                        Layered
"say" so mute, so nonsonant we
   winced, thick skin thinner
   the farther we went, thin skin
                        rubbed
away

SONG OF THE ANDOUMBOULOU: 30

So somewhere not the same I
strummed an n'goni, nonsonant strings
so introvert we wondered why
bother, by now no longer the we
who would. Arms lifted
                              winglike,
    ready, would we would fly,
      slack strings feathering the
    bones underneath, newly born
    sense we defeated doubt. . .
                              Spoke
      low, strict sticks' accompaniment.
    What limbs we'd given to get to
      it kept time, spooked feet
    spastic the faster we went,
                              legs
    taken away by cliff dirt,
                         the other
    world we were also in. . .
                              Told a
    cracked voice told it best, we cracked
      our voices, took nonsonance itself
    between our teeth, cracked its cover,
                              called
      it *Book of Disinterring the Book*. . .

Itch was our west, ambulacy our
    north, rasp eleven-sided, napped
on all sides, angled, endlessly
                         steeped. . .
    Entered leaving, elegiac from
    the start, Sophia said. Them
      again, I thought, shrugged it
                              off.
All the songs of the what-sayer's
      youth were on the box, Eronel the
    name he now called her, so much of
    what he said so distant, she
                         said,

she couldn't quite say what it
    was. . . East was an up-again
ladder, south a late wish it were
rungless. Airegin lay to our left. . .
    Adamant elsewhere conjured,
                                kept
after, kept alive, two-way-tending,
    backward-borne bent. Up was all
erasure, down a blunt stub,
                            where we
        were the music's where, nowhere
                                        to
be found. . .
                    He and Eronel lay side by
    side, he insisted. On their backs
        looking up at the sky, Rift
and Rescission,   might rift and
    rescission again lie so at
                                ease. . .
        Sound's promise of place fell
                                away,
        step taken off a cliff, rasp held
            onto like straw, Stra Precipice,
        Nudge, the non-world we were in,
                                        steep
    release

Though once we set out suppressed
resonance had its way, nonsonant
  head so hard it rang notwithstanding,
    sound so in advance of sense
                              we
  surrendered, whoosh rattling our teeth,
we were eating wind. The non-song we
    sang anansic, short of breath,
                              elegiac
    bone,   we walked along, hands deep
                              in our
      pockets, kicked rocks, long coats dragging the
      ground erased our footprints, Nudge
    the low rub we walked. . .

    So that what I wanted was to be
      made of what made sound recede into
    sough, Nudge repossess itself, be
      my birthright, Nonsonance
    lie next to Nudge, west of Nudge,
                              scratched
      inner skin's insistence. . . More than
      we could see or say we couldn't
    see, non-see's tongue taken over,
      deficit "say,"   cracked voice's
                              caw,
  stumbling
            strum

·

What it withheld was what we
heard, thought we heard, thought's
ear bent not by sound but by
    time-lapse,   lapse long wed
with tone were wood water,
    wed we would also be. . .
                        Albeit
  a balcony known as Nonsonant
    Serenade lay under our feet,
something we said we only dreamt we
  said, whatsaid arrival's
phantom wood might wood have known
  less restraint,   *World in retreat*
shouted out from windows and rooftops,
                      nonsonant
    nonetheless. . . Nonsonant world more
  real than any we'd expected. Loomed,
    lit by qu'ahttet light. . . We
lay on our backs looking up at
  the bottoms of ships, we
                 were under
  the sea. Pinched one another, soaked
    wood's awakening. Pinched wood
                 shivered,
  shook

•

A man made of wind and a woman
he said showed up unannounced. Zra
   people he proposed I be one
of, Zra movement be music,
                           Zra
   music. Holding air he was
   holding the world, he intimated,
     lolled his tongue, trailed
     off into singing, Lebert
                      Aaly
     the name he now took. . .
  Sought movement, markers of
     movement, tongues numb with
                           names
   not having moved. . .

  Came now to a place was more
time than place, nonsonant
   music's tipped acquittal,
  long-known place known as
By-and-By. . .
              We lay on
   our stomachs looking
  down at the ground.
                 A wall
we'd seen dirt sliding down lay
   to our right. Heard,
  though there was no sound,
   a suggestion of sound,
                  nonsonant
  sough slipped earth
contrived

Something said in my sleep
culled a deeper sleep. Deep
  dream's deeper say sewn
                    outward,
    "zigzag lightning" hit him he
  said, he insisted stiff nipples
      punctured his chest. A
    red-beaked bird pecked away
at the ark it turned out they
                    were on,
    wood what before had been
      iron, water what before had
                    been wood. . .
Eronel the name he now called her,
    nonsonant rut the what-sayer
  inferred they were stuck
      in, soul-boat, long-night
                    lunge. . .
  They lay on their sides looking
    into each other's eyes,
  scent of dry spit on their
      skins, having licked one
    another, held each other,
                    lidless,
    let go. . . Eronel's ribs were the
      strings he plucked, sophic
      strop, nonsonant lute rubbed
                    razorlike,
    rapt, skeletal
                strum

80

She no longer the she who'd
arrived unannounced, he no longer
    the he I'd been taken aside
by. Two we now saw sat watching
    videos of the dead, no
                            longer the
    two who'd put a shell to my ear.
So remote an approximation, poignant,
    told he'd mirror himself he
masked himself,   shell so buffed
    it vanished,   "polished"
        meant "passed away." Spoke
                            of an
    "it" which had become the tongue
    with which they spoke, whatsaid
        she whose heavy chest pressed
                            his. . .

    Mystic affliction, mystic remit,
        adamant imprint. . . Rose from
    it wanting it more, sweet
                        bewilderment,
        god what, godlike, seemed
                            so,

        gone

SONG OF THE ANDOUMBOULOU: 31

Sound was back. Bukka White
sang "Single Man Blues" on
the box, renamed it "Ogo's
    Lament." He and Eronel
lay chest to chest, right
                        leg
    to left. . . Some we met said
                        they were
    outmoded, failed andoumboulouous
birth brought back to life,
                        trek
    we resisted they insisted we
set out on, whatsaid hejira, what
    being said made so. . .

No what for which to've come, no
    why, lift we spoke of lost
as we spoke, nonsonant last
resort. So that all thought
    was now transitless "it,"
                        blunt
    would-be husk, maculate mask
turned iterative tooth, recidivist
gum,   feasted on scraps laid
    aside for some ghost.
    Skeletal he no less than
        skeletal she filled in
                        from
    memory. Skeletal they spun
        by skeletal we, backwardsbending
    rush. . . Skeletal stretch,
stretched limbs' analogic
        landscape, backwardswalking
                        vamp's
        lag-inducted run. . .

                        Me not
looking at them, them not looking
    at me, we stood looking out

across the wall which held us
                              back.
    Something unclear was being
        sung about a man who couldn't feel
        his toe, something we heard, thought
    we heard, said his neck
        had been cut. . . Nor could
                              we,
        having stood so long on
        the tips of our toes, nonsonant
                              struff
        the new ledge we
    walked

                    •

    Wanted to say of he-and-she-ness
    it creaks, bit our tongues,
        we who'd have been done with
                              him and her
        were we able, each the
                              other's
    legendary lack. Uninevitable
    he who'd have sooner been
    she, uninevitable she who'd
        have sooner been he. . .
                              We,
        who'd have been done
                              with both,
        looked out across the wall,
                              saw
        no new day
    come

Whatever it was we were
on. Wherever it was
we were. Elsewhere was
elsewhere, always. . . No way
we'd end up there. . .

                      Strung out
across the he/she line, we
relented, convinced it
was a train we were on.
Backwardswalking Lenore
looked us each in the
eye while receding, Eronel
the name we called her,
Monk's tune long taken
                  away. . .

So that love's newly
disengendered voice
coiled up from under
us, epithet as much as
elegy, we of whose
adamance much had
been made, fraught
voice too long
                  taken to,
loath under
                lifted
cloth

Who were drowning, dreaming it
seemed. "Because we don't need
    to be messed with," we said out
loud in our sleep, repeated
        it over and over, said why,
                                wouldn't
        say why what.
                        Burnt word
    we applauded, worlded us
        more than we knew. Myth
    asked had it been there would
        we have seen it,   wished-for
            resolution, resisted,
    the new day we said we
                            not-saw. . .
Wondered where the we we
    were after would come
from, awaited what rush
    we were told awaited
                        us,
    "beyond" but with what
    but skin to make a
    mark, high mind, high
        fractious mind
                    heart's
        meat

85

SONG OF THE ANDOUMBOULOU: 32

— low quadrant —

As if it were something they'd
read in a book, that it be
   their book, scrambling
               letters
as the word itself burned. . .
   Whatsaid book built on a
glimpse caught in passing.
   Something they saw,
              thought
   they saw, could only be
   told of in code. . .
            He her
star-specked haunches. She
   his rump-struck stare. . .
   Stood momentarily rungless,
             adamant
air all there was underfoot. . .
   Took the name of an Algerian
wine, Sidi Brahim. Meant by that
to announce a new rapture, aggregate
   air they found themselves
   taken up thru, loquat allure
            alive again
   as he spoke. . .
          Took me aside
   but spoke only in code. Taut
           cloth
held him back as he stretched,
shook as it dawned on him again what
   had happened,   rail he'd been
run into exile on, thin strip
          of world
   what was left. . . Mind adrift
   under Sophia's dress, fleetingness
   of thought tasting fruitlike
     pendance of cheek, heat wafting
          hoisted
rump. Was only one rung behind

as they climbed up the ladder,
head said to be in the clouds,
                              her
     pantyless ass only inches
     away. . . Rung number eight
     was the one he stood on,
                              rung
made of would-be, whim, wished
                              it were
     so, feet stuck on loquat wood. . .

                              Sophic
     butt, he blurted out, called it a
     setup. Called himself a bomb set
     to explode. . . Fuse and wick rolled
     into one, devilish,   dervish,
                              demiurgic
snuff. Belatedly reached for the strap
of her sandal, silhouetted leg, sunlit
     straw. . .   Took to singing. Wind and
regret rode his voice, a thin wine we
                              sipped,
     unspun. . .   Sophic body, trunk of
     a swing tree, a bottle hung from each
     of its branches, glass they looked in
     thru. Sidi Brahim was their see-thru
     mouthpiece, the he she'd have had them
                              speak
thru, glass mouth they blew into. . .
     No matter the outcome, loquat allure
lit their limbs, filled whatever
     crack it fell in. . . Adventitious
                              two
     lately known as Rift and Rescission,
                              wine what
     ran between

87

SONG OF THE ANDOUMBOULOU: 33

So bumpy a ride it was
we soon wanted out. We
were in Bahrain. "Marr
                              walaa
salaam," we heard. "They
    went by but didn't
    say salaam," someone
    said it meant, jook
                              song
    sung to oud accompaniment,
what they the singer chided
    chided him back. . .
Parsed out a retort, part
    praise, part taunt, a
    beginner again. "'Larger
                              what's
    lost to you,' they said,"
                              he sang,
    "Yesterday I stayed awake."
Whatsaid meeting, met with
    one who spoke of wisdom
as a hit, heft having much to
    do with it, hers whom he
                              called
    Anuncia, earlier having
    called her N'ahtt. . .

                              A cross
adorned her chest he'd been
    told. Envied it its address
of her cleavage, cleft he'd
    have pressed his face to
                              had he
been able,   rapt, irreligious,

88

                                    no jihad. . .
The we they'd have been,
                         dreamt
remnant it became, what
  we saw was all hearsay it
  seemed. Theirs the eventual
    audience's, not only his,
                                    hers. . .
  Audible wish to be seen. Taken
    eye turned on itself. . .
                              "Answered
  in kind, sighs alone would have
cracked our ribs," he heard her
      whisper, words he'd have
  whispered in turn had his
    tongue not stuck. . .
                                Theirs
      the cast-out, eventual
        crux, cornerstone. Stood
  as again she went by
        without speaking,
                              sang,
      "Went by without speaking,"
                                        out
    of reach

                    •

    Only what of it he could
  put into words could he
    rescind. Is remained is,
    implacable. Tree was
                          what its
        name would be, only were
        wood water, he her self-described
  apostle, hand cupping an abstract
    breast, wanting the
                            world. . .
  Ran to no end but to've
drifted somewhere distant,
    horse whose being ridden rode
  them both. . . Bedded
                    down

in a burnt-out house,
                              wicks lit
      to Ogun. Each a cracked
      egg, coaxed air, low-pitched
      ignition, hit by their
      below-the-belt abruptness,
                                 won
        by their below-the-waist
      allure. . . Said of that world,
                              about
        to leave it, so much less than
           we'd been led to expect.
      To've thought at all,
         thought of it as legged,
      what where there was reached
                                   only
        in thought, what reach remonstrant,
      strode as though lit within amber,
        andoumboulouous legs, fossilized
                                 light. . .
      So that the dreamthing we heard spoke
        thru more than one mouth.
                                 The
      Soon-Come Congress of Souls
           was now in session. Hafez
        blew a chicken-bone clarinet
                              he'd
      brought back from Iran. . . Dreamt
        writ calibrated our eclipse,
      whatsaid we. It was an out
           sound we echoed, broken branch
                                   we

        reckoned by

                    •

      Stra Hajj the path we took, roust
      what got us there. We who were the
        we they'd have been, dreamt
      concupiscence, the Soon-Come Congress
        no sooner there than
                              gone. . .
      Parts pulled apart, wandered,

Stra Palace the place they knew
next. . . An asthmatic wind infused
    what floor lay under them.
                          Nay
was what their name would be,
                          Zra's
    raw-throated flute. . . Words
don't go there, they said,
    no sooner said than they were
        there, albeit there defied location. . .
    City they'd been told they'd someday
                              get to,
        eventual city known as By-and-By. . .
That there was a war going
    on they'd forgotten,
                      "Blues
    for the Fallen" on the box
        notwithstanding, rapt,
                          remnant
    heat the one flame
they saw

Antiphon Island's imagined
mooring, albeit marooned we
took it she'd be. Left-hand
insinuance had its way with
her, hailed her, halted
                              her,
hauled her in. . . Held up her thumb
    and forefinger, all but
touching. Scrunched an eye as
if to look between. "If it
could only be gotten that flat,"
                              she
        said, "compressed, all would be
    ours again." Dawn after dawn
    announced, *On this night. . . Tonight
at noon. . .* , see-thru cloth housing an
outline of legs in black tights,
                    cloth she'd
    have made a new world of, thread such as
        he whose work was otherwise relinquished,
    more than he'd been led to expect. . .

    Nobody's fool. Nobody's majnoun. Nowhere
        near taken up as she'd have been,
    said she'd been, more than he'd
        been led to expect, let himself
    expect, stranded, washed ashore on
                              Lone
Coast

92

Another he, no longer the same
though related. She, of whom
the same could be said. . .
                          An asthmatic
    wind underneath it all, Hoarse
Chorus, they who were the would-be
    we she projected, hand so abruptly
out from under her dress, her
    sniffed finger's lewd
                          report. . .
Lifted a finger she'd brushed
        her loins with   up to
    above his upper lip,
                          whispered,
        "Attar," that this would
come back to him again and
    again come back to him,
                          more
than he could make any sense
                          of, abrupt
    move the abrasive nay so
insisted on, seemed it
    so insisted on, only,
                  even
so

•

And so told us how far it was
though we thought it,
                              return
to Stra Palace, Jah Hajj.
                              Madame
    Zzaj the name she now took
        to be done with naming,
                              names
    no longer slide might such be
so. . .
        A sudden rain, so we ducked
        under leaves. Wood became shed,
                              meaning
Tree. Trunk, unembraceable,
                              beckoned,
    wide girth we'd have given the
        world to've been one with, run
                              with, roots
    above ground

94

Stra Hajj was behind us now.
It seemed it was a train we
were on, church we were
                            in,
stuck voices all but
tugged us down. . .
Plucked strings made the
floorboards buckle, tenuous
                            hold on
what we had more tenuous.
                            Hoarse
Chorus the congress of souls
we exacted,   soul serenade,
                            whatsaid
surmount. . .
                So that the he
we heard sing stayed
with us, haunted
us, allowed us to move
like music,
                but in
boxcars, hobos it
                seemed

95

Runaway band run out of
Rast on a rail, rail band. . .
Rail meant romance, removal,
                                    to at
        last have been done with
        waiting, else the awaited
        where run come. . .
                            Rast
            meant far, Stra farther,
        for all espousal to the
            contrary called it
                            Star. . .
        Strewn relation, relinquishment,
                more than any one way
    reckoned,   weird what we
        took to be movement,
                                    moored
        where we took it
    we'd left

SONG OF THE ANDOUMBOULOU: 33½

Low, ushering blast at our backs
as we leapt on. . .

So bumpy a ride our knitcaps
    unraveled. . .

    Blinded by what before we
not-saw. Crouched in a shot-up
    room in Chicago, cops in a
                    circle
outside. As if to've died and
    come back as birds, hollow
bones blown flutelike, Flutter
for now our name, next now
                forever
not yet, as if stuck some imagined
              where
    we could only allude to. . .
            Rags.
    Recollected Stra. . .

Low hang of hip. Plump
    handful of heaven.
           As if,
    world as it was, what better
    balm than remembered
    caresses, Ornette's
"Embraceable You" on the
           box
    though there was no
box, gruff thrum treading
    the air. . . Runaway
          band
run out of where we
    were, name no longer
Flutter, now Flight. . .
        So
    that what the what-sayer
said relieved us, though

of what not even we
                              could
say

What we rode was a boat he
  lay on whose deck looking out
from, boat caught in qu'ahttet
    light. Onerous ghost of an
                                    Egyptian
  beginning. . . Tenuous union. . .
                                Oneiric
    regret. . . Uninhabited groom to
the hand he'd have touched her
  with, gripped "it" emptied into
  the underness of her dress, dreamt
and emptied "it" gripped and let
                          go. . .
  He lay on his back recollecting
what had been, glimpse drawn out
  into endlessness, the new and old
    wonder they wore nothing
                          underneath,
    Anuncia's neck sweating but sweet,
      salty-sweet,   Anuncia drew
    his tongue to her neck. Raised
      her hand and would be her own
  witness, backwardswalking, two-headed
  twin, one head would be Eronel, the
                                other
  Lenore. . . Vaunted loveliness, vaunted
    allure. Vaunted flesh lately
  dubbed House of Bones. . . House they'd
    eventually exit, she insisted, sooner
      not be seen, she said. . . An alternate
    house posed on bamboo flute bore sophic
                                    stir,
proffered body all but available,
                    vexed. . .

  They lay in our boat looking out at
the earth, flat but for the relief
  love gave it. They lay on their backs
looking out at the sky. Whatever it was it

was a boat we were on, bus we were
on, sat on a train orbiting abject
                                    Earth. . .
    Attended by two who'd wandered away
among those who got off to pee, arkical
    city soon to be founded we thought,
glimpse gotten of God under loquat
                                    leaves. . .
    That it wasn't there or that it was
but unreachable,   hard to say
    which was worse,   the Soon-Come
Congress no sooner come than gone, train
    we thought we'd asked how long about,
                                    minds

    ever only half there.   Linked arms,
we whose hands held only *Gimme*, gone
    but for the look of arrival, whose
hot mouths hawked *Much obliged*. . .
                                    Suddenly
    walked on newly collected limbs, agitant
    legs beneath abrasive cloth. . . Off to
our left, bright sea of strings, bounce of
    light off the water blinding us, more
                                    than we
could see but saw. . . Would-be train we'd
    heard about in sermons, songs,   to ride
    was to bid exile goodbye. Ride meant to
    be done with waiting, swung to one
side though we were, then the other,
                                    swung
    short of boated, bussed. . .

                                    Stepped out of
    the car so that now it was a car we'd
been in. Stepped, stood on the side
    of the road, stepped and shivered, met
by newly arctic wind. Stowaway gust caught
in fallen cloth. Gnostic sleeper stowed
                                    away on
    the boat we rode, runaway sunship, Trane's
namesake music's runaway ghost. . .
                                    Posthumous
    music made us almost weep, wander,

100

Soon-Come Congress we'd otherwise have
 been, sung to if not by Lenore by
                                    Eronel,
 every which way, on our way
                        out

Said by some to have been its own
extenuance, sameness no longer
itself, subtly altered, said to
    have lain with itself. Low
                      circular
   song lamenting flight, frustration,
                     so
    tightly entwined an andoumboulouous two
  into which it split, each the other's
    whatsaid rut. . . Lay on their
backs imagining Nut bent over them,
                      starred
   arch the sun's boat absconded on. . .
Absent body. . . Recondite warmth. . .
                 We lay
  on our backs imagining them imagining
                    us,
  andoumboulouous twins turned qu'ahttet
                   complement,
   pan-pronominal choir,
            ythmic
remit

So now knew Stray lay west of
Stra. Out was a balafonic bridge,
   its beat our boat, bedouin wind
wandered so far north we shook,

                              shivered,
   boated out of Ahtt we'd have been had
   we been able, gone against our
   will out of Ttha. . . Wherever we
      were there was an elsewhere we

                           were,
      gruff alterity rosining the cords
of our throats,   blank but for
   the grain we gave it, swift glimpse
   gone atthic, apocryphal, epiphanous,

                              map
drawn on snatched-away straw. *Scatter be*
   my name, something said, more sough
than say, dreamt insinuance it turned out
   to be albeit real, rubbed against our

                              faces,
      raw. Freight of wind and of waywardness,
      atlessness, drift,   draped and enjambed

                           hasp of
      heaven, short of heaven, moot condolences
coaxed out of stricken wood. . . Sea of
   strings to our left yet again, symphonic
shimmer, posthumous music all the more
   poignant, putative soul-boat, southern

                           sky. . .
Left of Nonsonance we turned as the
box got back its voice,   regaled
   us with tales of lost ground gotten

                              back,
      crooned of lost love rewon. But we
were beyond it, bleak skeleton crew on
   the boat we rode, subtly in front,

                           phantom
   projection, southern
                     prow

Wept adhesion, the way of the Kaluli.
Remanent water, whatsaid salt. . .
Whatsaid rise into inclement wind,
                              blown
abrasion, whatsaid book of undoing the
book. Scratched voice the near side of
    silence, a writing before writing
                              writing's
work was to announce, scorched air scoured,
                              scuffed. . .
    Rough, andoumboulouous draft whose we
they were, who lay on their backs wrapped in
    burlap it seemed. Rough weave
    and as rough an unwinding,
                              rough
turn finding themselves so drawn. . .
                              Tropic
    wind out of nowhere, world a magnetic
                              rock,
clung to, the better to be let go, they
    insisted, beginning, they said again,
                              to
    say goodbye

In Wrack Tavern we raised our glasses,
drank to how far they'd come. Distant
    kin long dead brought to life by the
    wine we sipped, revenant dead said
                                    to've
        died or been dying of thirst. . .
    Clink of glass, clink of chains
        transmuted. Andoumboulouous trauma,
andoumboulouous launch. Boat of years,
    black-orphic lament, boat of
                            yearning. . .
        The nay-player's dilated nostril,
    adventitious odor only music
    addressed. . . So that hoarseness
                            bore the
Ahtt we were after, Ttha the most abstract
                            "at"
        we'd ever inhabit, tossed, low-throated
                                perfume,
    weathered fret, window
        ever out of
Ahtt's reach

Sun cult.　　Cargo cult.　　Pharaoh's
Andalusian song our secret cargo, the
sun burning a hole in the sky. . .
　　　　　　　　　　　　　　The voice
was a boat where there'd be no boat.
No balm, no abdominal blessing, unless the
voice draw the torso up. . . Abdominal
　　　　　　　　　　　　　　　　scuff
and impatient loin-rut. . . Ache and orexic
　　　　　　　　　　　　　　　　trunk
sung from under. . . Hoist and thoracic
struff. . .

Dreamt beginning. Unbased
itch and intransigence. . .
　　　　　　　　　　End
urged inside
out

SONG OF THE ANDOUMBOULOU: 35

A last meeting after other
last meetings. Up what felt
  like a stairway a window at
  which he sat overlooking
                              Lone
      Coast, his eyes' and the
      water's color the inside
        color of green grapes. . .
  A last meeting. Another last
      meeting. Now in a mood
                              where
        if I said "struck" he
                          said "stricken,"
        the sound a song of wanting
      to have risen, flute-borne abrasion
      a sudden flight of stairs newly
                                  right
  side up. Where we had gone or what we
      had gotten. . . What the soul, again
  said to have been a boat or been
      on a boat, grew wings and went
      down on all fours to go after,
                                      cracked
  alterity,   qu'ahttet kin. . . Up what
      felt like a stairway a window at
      which he sat looking out at Lone
                                  Coast.
  Sat myself down beside him. The
  nay-player sat beside me. . .

      Whatsaid remanence. Whatsaid
      remit. What the nay said's
                              whatsaid
      quaver, clipped reed an asthmatic
      embankment, reach if not roll of it
      missed by the names we knew it
  by,   Brush,   Blown Host,   Ramp
                                          of
      Heaven. . . All to say a ghost

had shown up we knew by more than
one name, Ahtt being not yet
erased, rearranged, rearrangement's
                              intimated
    eclipse. What, unaffected by
                          in-between,
    inside was outside would be, wished
    it would be, said it would be, said
    wish made so. . . Spooked amanuensis. . .
        Atthic recluse. . . Sat beside him,
                                  said
        only, "So." As if "So" summed everything
up, it seemed I sighed. *Would I were the*
    he they took me for, it seemed I said,
    semisaid, half-said, half-sang. . .
    I read from a book. I said only,
                              "So."

The Book of Iridescent Dissolve it
    seemed it was, bridge between "end"
and "again" he seemed intent on,
    brine book, nay-strewn salt. . .
    I said only, "So." "So" said it
                          all. . .
    All there was to say went skyward,
    thin ventriloquial smoke. What it
seemed I said, semisaid, it seemed he
                              wrote. . .

    It was a green book we made, yellow
book, red book, black tablet we
scratched in Wrack Tavern. Bits of
                              mirror
        made it flash, fade, flash again,
    strobelit, ythmic writ. A twist
        of cloth or an appurtenance of
        straw bore gnostic import, known,
it was ours to infer, by none if
                          not by
    those who no longer spoke. . .
        Inductees into a school of scramble,
        the altered state we rode in search of
                              receding,
    Emanon the something-out-of-nothing
we saw

•

Sat straddling two extremes. Endlessly
gave names to what had none. One foot
on Lookout Ledge, the other on Loquat
Lift, flute furtherance a bank of mulled
                                        air
    we came to next, mulled air posed
    as atavistic earth. . . Another meeting
    which was another last meeting. Sat in
Qua Precipice's open-air café, looked
                                   out on
        Lone Coast. Yet again spoke of his
        Lady of the Loquat Tree. . . Claimed
        she had forgotten more than we knew,
                                         knew
    more than we knew, not known for knowing,
        the train, bus, boat we'd been on
    long borne away, said flute furtherance
    ate away at Lookout Ledge. His was an
                                     I hers
    ignited, he insisted, theirs had it
                                been his
        to give. . . All to say that two no longer
with us long ago lay side by side,
                                    each
    the other's ordained exit each of them
    thought, there though if only in thought no
        less to be reckoned with, each
                                     the
other's elegiac twin. So to say that we
                                   whose
        flutes blew elsewhere weakened, they
        whose we approached revived, mythic
        repair borne by nothing if not by
                                     breath
    we took, nonsonance's nay-splayed
                                   scut.
        Whatsaid ride into a realm of silence.
        There was a word we were told to keep
        to ourselves. . . The word was rapture and
    it stuck in our throats, whose last resort,
                                           we
        heard it said, was to be so
taken

109

Name Ad Nauseam stood in our way, was
our way, loquat coinage's wind-affianced
escort, exodus, flute-furthered,
qu'ahttet flight. At the sound of its
                              blowing
    we bowed our heads, he who'd have been
        otherwise, we who were not. . .
                                  Hung
        in the air at Tbal's behest, we
            who'd been birds whose heads grew to
            such music, hoofed instruction
                                  borne
    by Abakwa drums. . .
                          Repeatedly scratched
        at the paper we wrote on, Stra Choir's
        laryngitic address. . .
                          Flute furtherance's
        culled undercurrent, stuck surrogacy,
                                      felt
        for the level on which to fade, utterly
                                      placeless,
    skulls rapped by knuckles, aggregate
                              fist

Echoed an earlier echo. . . "Cuando
yo me muera," semisaid, semisung,
   cante jondo's bluff. . . "When I die,"
we half-said, half-sang. Worm in
                              our throats,
      inexistent smoke it came out of.
   Shook what could be said to've
      housed it, dream within a dream,
   fraught forfeiture, fret. . .
                        Cramped
         expanse we crossed, came to
      Qua Precipice. A green book,
         red book, yellow, painted
      scroll, read as we rode
                        it seemed. . .
         Stubbled earth an extended
         braille we redacted, blind,
                              ythmic
      rush, limbic
   strum

Photo by Paul Schraub

Nathaniel Mackey, recipient of a 1993 Whiting Writer's Award, is the author of *Bedouin Hornbook, Eroding Witness, School of Udhra, Discrepant Engagement: Dissonance, Cross-Culturality, and Experimental Writing,* and *Djibot Baghostus's Run.* He teaches literature at the University of California at Santa Cruz.